Scholastic Success With
Reading Comprehension
Grade 1

by Robin Wolfe

W9-BDM-611

S C H O L A S T I C
PROFESSIONAL BOOKS

**New York • Toronto • London • Auckland • Sydney •
Mexico City • New Delhi • Hong Kong • Buenos Aires**

Cover art by Victoria Raymond
Cover design by Maria Lilja
Interior illustrations by Kathy Marlin
Interior design by Quack & Company

ISBN 0-439-044489-6

Copyright © 2002 Scholastic, Inc.
All rights reserved. Printed in the U.S.A.

11 12   40   09 08

Introduction

Parents and teachers alike will find **Reading Comprehension** to be a valuable learning tool. Children will enjoy reading a wide variety of stories that are humorous or informative. The activities include puzzles and other fun ways of finding answers and are tools for improving comprehension skills. Finding the main idea, reading for details, drawing conclusions, and following directions are just some of the skills included. First graders are also challenged to develop vocabulary, identify cause and effect, and analyze characters. They are encouraged to try different reading strategies that will help them become better readers. Take a look at the Table of Contents. You will feel rewarded providing such a valuable resource for your children.

Remember to praise children for their efforts and successes!

Table of Contents

Tim Can Read

Tim is a good reader.
He uses clues to help him read.
First, he looks at the picture.
That helps him know what the
story is about. Next, he reads the
title of the story. Now he knows a
little more. As he reads the story,
the words make pictures in his mind.

Color in the book beside the correct answer.

1. Who is Tim?

 a good reader   a math whiz

2. What does Tim do first?

 reads the story   looks at the picture

3. What else helps Tim know what the story will be about?

 the title   the page number

4. As he reads, what makes pictures in Tim's mind?

 the letters   the words

Now you can try reading the stories in this book the way that Tim does. If you do, you will be
a good reader, too! Write the name of your favorite book here.

Scholastic Professional Books

Trucks

 *The **main idea** tells what the whole story is about.*

Trucks do important work. Dump trucks carry away sand and rocks. Cement trucks have a barrel that turns round and round. They deliver cement to workers who are making sidewalks. Fire trucks carry water hoses and firefighters. Gasoline is delivered in large tank trucks. Flatbed trucks carry wood to the people who are building houses.

Find the sentence in the story that tells the main idea. Write it in the circle below. Then draw a line from the main idea to all the trucks that were described in the story.

 Write the sentence that tells the main idea on another sheet of paper. Draw a picture that tells about the sentence.

Circus Clowns

➡ The **main idea** *tells what the whole story is about.*

Today I went to the circus. My favorite part of the circus was the clowns. Clowns can do funny tricks. A clown named Pinky turned flips on the back of a horse. Fancy Pants juggled balls while he was singing a funny song. Happy Hal made balloons into animal shapes. Then twelve clowns squeezed into a tiny car and rode away.

Color in the ball that tells the main idea.

Pinky rides a horse.

Balloons can be shaped like animals.

Clowns can do funny tricks.

Clowns drive tiny cars.

Fancy Pants sang a song.

Your Name

When you were born, your parents thought of a name for you. You might be named after someone in the family. Maybe you were named after a movie star! Almost every name has a meaning. Pamela means *honey*. Henry means *master of the house*. Ellen means *bright*. Sometimes books about baby names tell the meanings. Many of the meanings will surprise you!

Circle the name below that has the main idea of the story in it.

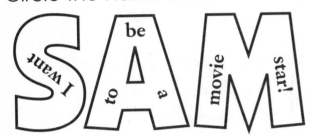

To find out the meanings of the names in the puzzle below, follow each string of beads. Copy the letters on each bead in order in the boxes.

Casey means

George means

Sarah means

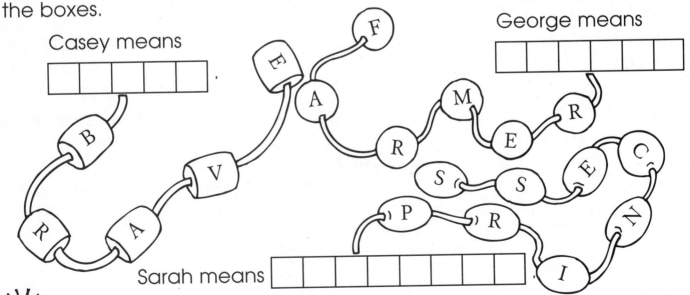

 Read a book to someone at home at bedtime. Tell the main idea of the story.

Striped Critters

Details *are parts of a story. Details help you understand what the story is about.*

Skunks are small animals that live in the woods. They have black fur with one or two white stripes down their backs. Bugs are their favorite food. They also eat mice. If a skunk raises its tail, run away! Skunks can spray a very smelly liquid at anyone who bothers them.

Write the answers in the crossword puzzle.

Across:

2. What color are the stripes on a skunk's fur?

5. What is a skunk's favorite food?

Down:

1. What is another thing that skunks like to eat?

2. Where do skunks live?

3. What does a skunk raise when it is getting ready to spray?

4. What should you do if a skunk raises its tail?

 Use details to describe your favorite animal.

Scholastic Professional Books

Ricky's Wish

Details *are parts of a story. Details help you understand what the story is about.*

Ricky loved to go camping. One day during reading class, he began to daydream about camping in the mountains. He thought about going fishing and riding horses. It would be fun to gather logs to build a campfire and cook hot dogs. He and his dad could set up the tent near some big trees. He wished he were in his canoe right now. Just then, Ricky heard his teacher say, "Ricky, it is your turn to read." Oh no! He had lost the place!

Circle these things from the story hidden in the picture below: a fish, a fishing pole, a log for the campfire, a hot dog, a tree, and a canoe.

1. Where was Ricky during this story? _____

_____

2. Where would Ricky like to have been? _____

_____

What do you like to daydream about? Write about it using details.

Going to Grammy's

Kelly is going to spend the night with her grandmother. She will need to take her pajamas, a shirt, and some shorts. Into the suitcase go her toothbrush, toothpaste, and hairbrush. Grammy told her to bring a swimsuit in case it was warm enough to swim. Mom said to pack her favorite pillow and storybooks. Dad said, "Don't forget to take Grammy's sunglasses that she left here last week." Now Kelly is ready to go!

1. Color the things that Kelly packed in her suitcase.

2. A compound word is a big word that is made up of two little words. For example, cow + boy = cowboy. Find 8 compound words in this story and circle them.

On the back of this page, make a list of things you would pack if you were going to spend the night at your grandmother's house.

George W. Bush

George W. Bush grew up in Texas. When he finished college, he worked in the oil business. Later on, he became the governor of Texas, then the 43rd president of the United States. His wife's name is Laura. They have twin daughters named Jenna and Barbara. The Bush family owns a ranch in Texas. They have two dogs named Barney and Spotty.

The Bush family also has a cat. To find out the name of their cat, write the answers in the blanks. Then copy the letters that are in the shapes into the empty shapes below.

1. Mr. Bush grew up in ___ ___ ___ ___ ___ .

2. He worked in the ___ ___ ___ business.

3. He became the 43rd ___ ___ ___ ___ ___ ___ ___ ___ ___
   of the United States.

4. Laura Bush is Mr. Bush's ___ ___ ___ ___ .

5. Mr. Bush's daughters are Barbara and ___ ___ ___ ___ .

His cat's name is ___ ___ ___ ___ ___

 If you were president of the United States, what new law would you make? Write it in a complete sentence, including three details.

Mr. Lee's Store

 *Story events that can really happen are **real**. Story events that are make-believe are **fantasy**.*

At night, Mr. Lee locked the store and went home. That's when the fun began! The ketchup bottles stood in rows like bowling pins. Then the watermelon rolled down the aisle and knocked them down. The chicken wings flew around the room. Cans of soup stacked themselves higher and higher until they laughed so hard that they tumbled over. Carrots danced with bananas. Then it was morning. "Get back in your places!" called the milk jug. "Mr. Lee is coming!" Mr. Lee opened the door and went right to work.

Circle the cans that are make-believe.

ketchup bottles and a watermelon bowling

a talking milk jug

dancing bananas

chicken wings that can fly all by themselves

Mr. Lee went to work.

laughing soup cans

Mr. Lee went home at night.

dancing carrots

a grocery store

 Draw a picture of the story on another piece of paper.

Cool Clouds

Have you ever looked up in the sky and seen a cloud that is shaped like an animal or a person? Big, white, puffy clouds float along like soft marshmallows. In cartoons, people can sit on clouds and bounce on them. But clouds are really just tiny drops of water floating in the air. You can understand what being in a cloud is like when it is foggy. Fog is a cloud on the ground!

Read each sentence below. If the sentence could really happen, color the cloud blue. If the sentence is make-believe, color it orange.

Clouds float in the sky.

A cartoon dog sleeps on a cloud.

Clouds are made of tiny drops of water.

Animal shapes in clouds are made by the Cloud Fairy.

Clouds are big blobs of whipped cream.

Clouds are made of marshmallows.

Fog is a cloud on the ground.

Birds can hop around on clouds.

Draw a picture to show a real cloud. Then draw a make-believe cloud.

Ready for School

 Sequencing *means putting the events in a story in the order they happened.*

Tara could hardly wait for school to start. Mom drove her to the store to buy school supplies. They bought pencils, crayons, scissors, and glue. When Tara got home, she wrote her name on all of her supplies. She put them in a paper sack. The next day, Tara went to school, but the principal told her and the other children to go back home. A water leak had flooded the building. Oh no! Tara would have to wait another whole week!

Number the pictures in the order that they happened in the story.

Color the supplies that Tara bought.

Swimming Lessons

 Sequencing *means putting the events in a story in the order they happened.*

Last summer I learned how to swim. First, the teacher told me to hold my breath. Then I learned to put my head under water. I practiced kicking my feet. While I held on to a float, I paddled around the pool. Next, I floated to my teacher with my arms straight out. Finally, I swam using both my arms and my legs. I did it! Swimming is fun! This summer, I want to learn to dive off the diving board.

Number the pictures in the order that they happened in the story.

Unscramble the letters to tell what the person in the story wants to do next.

EALNR   **OT**   **IVDE**

_____ _____ _____ _____ _____   _____ _____   _____ _____ _____ _____

 What would you like to learn to do? Draw four pictures on the back of your paper to show how to do it.

The Robin's Nest

  Words like first, then, next, *and* finally *help tell the* **sequence** *of a story.*

Read each sentence on the puzzle pieces below. Cut the pieces out along the black lines. When you put the story pieces together in order, the edges will match to make a shape. Glue the pieces onto another piece of paper. Then read the story again.

Finally, she laid her eggs in the nest.

Then she took the grass and straw to a tree branch.

The robin wanted to build a nest.

First, she found some grass and straw.

Next, she put the grass and straw together to make a nest.

Name _____

Shapes in the Sky

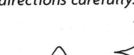 Be sure to read directions carefully.

Follow the directions.

1. Outline each star with a blue crayon. Then color each one red.

2. Color one moon yellow. Color the other one orange.

3. Draw a face on every sun.

4. Write the number of stars inside the star.

5. Write the number of moons inside the moon.

6. Write the number of suns inside the sun

7. Add the three numbers you wrote together to find the total number of shapes.

    _____ + _____ + _____ = _____

8. Which two shapes belong in the night sky?

    _____ and _____

 Draw a picture of the sun with nine planets around it. Write EARTH on our planet.

My Monster

 Be sure to read directions carefully. Look for key words like circle, underline, and color.

I saw a scary monster who lived in a cave. He had shaggy fur and a long, striped tail. He had ugly, black teeth. His three horns were shaped like arrows. His nose was crooked. One of his feet was bigger than the other three. "Wake up! Time for breakfast," Mom said. Oh, good! It was only a dream.

Follow the directions.

1. What did the monster's tail look like? Circle it.

2. What did the monster's teeth look like? Draw a box around them.

3. What did the monster's horns look like? Color them green.

4. What did the monster's nose look like? Underline it.

  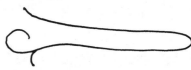

5. What did the monster's feet look like? Color them red.

  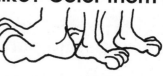 

6. Which one of these is the correct picture of the monster? Draw a cave around him.

Fun at the Beach

Jack and Joni went to the beach today. Mom spread a blanket on the sand, and they had a picnic. It got very hot, so Jack and Joni jumped into the cold water. They climbed onto a big yellow raft. The waves made the raft go up and down. Later, they played in the sand and built sandcastles. Jack and Joni picked up pretty shells. Joni found a starfish. What a fun day!

1. Color the pictures below that are from the story. Put an X on the ones that don't belong.

2. In the third sentence, find two words that are opposites of each other and circle them with a red crayon.

3. In the fifth sentence, find two more words that are opposites of each other and circle them with a blue crayon.

4. Draw a box around the compound word that tells what Joni found.

5. What color was the raft? Show your answer by coloring the picture at the top of the page.

 Write three sentences that tell how to get ready to play your favorite sport.

My New Rug

 When you use your own thoughts to answer the question, "How could that have happened?", you are drawing conclusions.

I bought a fancy rug today. It was made of brightly-colored yarn. I placed it on the floor in front of the TV and sat on it. All of a sudden, it lifted me up in the air! The rug and I flew around the house. Then out the door we went. High above the trees, we soared like an eagle. Finally, it took me home, and we landed in my backyard.

How could that have happened? To find out, use your crayons to trace over each line. Use a different color on each line. Write the letter from that line in the box at the bottom of the rug.

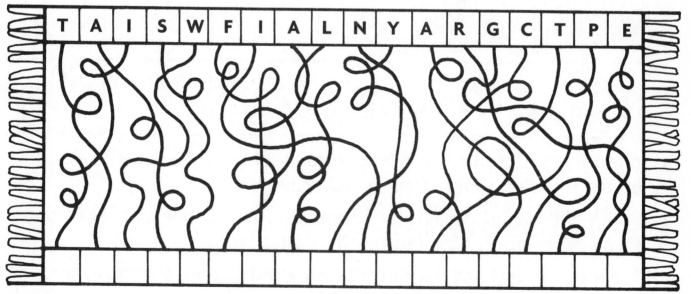

| T | A | I | S | W | F | I | A | L | N | Y | A | R | G | C | T | P | E |

Could this story really happen? Draw a rug around your answer.

Yes   **No**

 You left your ball on the steps. Your mother came down the steps carrying the laundry basket. Draw a picture of what you think happened.

Scholastic Professional Books

Polly Want a Cracker?

Have you ever heard a parrot talk? Parrots are able to copy sounds that they hear. You can train a parrot to repeat words, songs, and whistles. But a parrot cannot say words that it has never heard. People can use words to make new sentences, but a parrot cannot.

Read each sentence. If it is true, color the parrot under True. If it is false, color the parrot under False.

True   False

1. You could teach a parrot to sing "Happy Birthday."

2. You could ask a parrot any question, and it could give the answer.

3. A parrot could make up a fairy tale.

4. If a parrot heard your mom say, "Brush your teeth," every night, he could learn to say it, too.

5. It is possible for a parrot to repeat words in Spanish.

Write what would happen if a parrot heard you say, "No, I can't" too often.

You Be the Artist

 Picturing a story can help the reader understand it better.

An artist drew the pictures that are in this book. Now it is your turn to be the artist! Read each sentence very carefully. Draw exactly what you read about in the sentence.

1. **The green and yellow striped snake wiggled past the ants.**

2. **Wildflowers grew along the banks of the winding river.**

3. **On her sixth birthday, Shannon had a pink birthday cake shaped like a butterfly.**

 Now write your own sentence and illustrate it.

Scholastic Professional Books

A Stormy Day

Big, black clouds appeared in the sky. Lightning struck the tallest tree. The scared cow cried, "Moo!" It rained hard. Soon there was a mud puddle by the barn door. Hay blew out of the barn window.

Read the story above. Then go back and read each sentence again. Add to the picture everything that the sentences describe.

Who Am I?

 Use details from the story to make decisions about the characters.

Circle the picture that answers the riddle.

1. I have feathers. I also have wings, but I don't fly. I love to swim in icy water. Who am I?

2. I am 3 weeks old. I drink milk. I cry when my diaper is wet. Who am I?

3. I live in the ocean. I swim around slowly, looking for something to eat. I have six more arms than you have. Who am I?

4. I am an insect. If you touch me, I might bite you! I make tunnels under the ground. I love to come to your picnic! Who am I?

5. I am a female. I like to watch movies and listen to music. My grandchildren love my oatmeal cookies. Who am I?

6. I am a large mammal. I live in the woods. I have fur. I stand up and growl when I am angry. Who am I?

7. I wear a uniform. My job is to help people. I ride on a big red truck. Who am I?

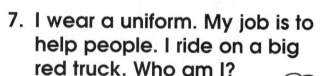 **Write your own riddle and let the class guess the answer.**

Scholastic Professional Books

What's Going On?

 Use story details to help you make decisions about the story.

James was the first boy in Miss Lane's class to find red spots on his face and arms. He scratched until his mom came to take him home. A week later, Amy and Jana got the spots. The next Monday, six more children were absent. Finally, everyone got well and came back to school. But, this time Miss Lane was absent. Guess what was wrong with her!

Color red spots on the correct answers.

1. What do you think was wrong with the children?

sore throats   chickenpox   broken arms

2. How do you know the spots were itchy?

James scratched them.

Amy said, "These spots itch!"

3. How many children in all got sick?

 2   5    9    4

4. Why do you think Miss Lane was absent? Write your answer.

_____

 Draw a picture of what Miss Lane might look like with chickenpox!

Make a Cartoon

Read the sentence below each picture. In the bubbles, write what each character could be saying.

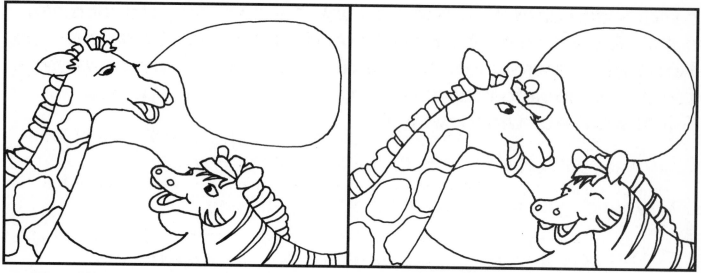

Mr. Giraffe asked Mr. Zebra why he had stripes. Mr. Zebra didn't know.

Mr. Giraffe said that he should ask Mrs. Owl. Mr. Zebra agreed.

Mr. Zebra asked Mrs. Owl why he had stripes. Mrs. Owl laughed.

Mrs. Owl told Mr. Zebra that the Magic Fairy painted him that way!

 If Mr. Giraffe asked Mrs. Owl why he had such a long neck, what do you think she would say?

Scholastic Professional Books

Name _____

Clean Your Room

 Grouping like things together makes it easier to remember what you read.

Mom says, "Let's go out for ice cream! Clean your room, and then we will go." Your room is a mess. You need to put the blocks in the basket. The crayons must go in their box. The books must go on the shelf, and the marbles go in the jar. You can do it. Just think about that hot fudge sundae!

Draw a line from each item on the floor to the place it belongs. Color what you could use in school red. Color what are toys blue.

Circle the food that does not belong in an ice cream store.

 Fold a sheet of paper in half. Write "hot" on one side and "cold" on the other side. Draw four foods on each side of the paper that go with the heading.

Scholastic Professional Books

Going to the Mall

 Look for similarities when grouping items.

Read the words in the Word Box. Write each word in the place where you would find these things at the mall.

Word Box

tickets	sandals	high heels	beans	big screen
tulip bulbs	peppers	fertilizer	popcorn	gardening gloves
sneakers	burritos	boots	pots	candy	tacos

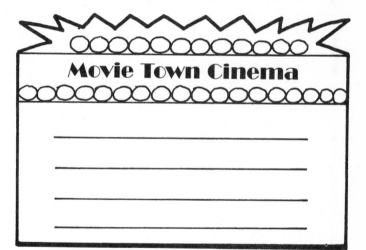

Sandie's Shoe Store

_____

_____

_____

_____

Movie Town Cinema

_____

_____

_____

_____

PEPE'S MEXICAN FOOD

_____

_____

_____

_____

Gale's Gardening Goodies

_____

_____

_____

_____

 On another sheet of paper, draw the following items in a toy store or a clothing store: jump rope, blue jeans, basketball, doll, sweatshirt, stocking cap, wooden train, pajamas.

Scholastic Professional Books

Are You Hungry?

Eating good food helps you grow up to be strong and healthy. There are many kinds of foods. Ham, chicken, and beef are meats. Dairy foods include milk, cheese, and yogurt. What kinds of bread do you like? I like rolls, bagels, and biscuits. Fruits and vegetables, such as carrots, corn, and apples, are good for you. They are full of vitamins.

Cut out the signs and the food pictures. Make a chart on another piece of paper. First, glue the signs at the top of the paper. Then, under each sign, glue the pictures that belong in each category.

Meats	Dairy	Breads

Fruits and Vegetables

When you are finished, draw another food in each category.

Scholastic Professional Books

Ouch!

 Use story details to make a guess of what will happen next.

Mia and Rosa were playing hospital. Mia was the patient, and Rosa was the doctor. Rosa pretended to take Mia's temperature. "You have a fever," she said. "You will have to lie down." Mia climbed onto the top bunk bed. "You need to sleep," Dr. Rosa said. Mia rolled over too far and fell off the top bunk. "O-o-o-h, my arm!" yelled Mia. Her mother came to look. It was broken!

What do you think happened next? Write your answer here.

_____

To find out if your answer is correct, finish the sentence below by coloring only the spaces that have a dot in them.

Mia had to go to

 If Mia hadn't fallen off the bed, how do you think this story would have ended? Draw your answer.

Scholastic Professional Books

What Will Sam Do?

One day, Sam was riding his bike to the baseball game. He had to be on time. He was the pitcher. Just ahead, Sam saw a little boy who had fallen off his bike. His knee was bleeding, and he was crying. Sam asked him if he was okay, but the boy couldn't speak English. Sam knew the boy needed help getting home. If he stopped to help, he might be late for the game. Sam thought about it. He knew he had to do the right thing.

What do you think Sam did next? There are two paths through the maze. Draw a line down the path that shows what you think Sam did next.

What sentence from the story gives you a hint about what Sam decided to do? Write that sentence below.

_____

 The maze shows two ways the story could end. Draw a different ending to the story and tell about your picture.

Riddle Fun

Compare *means to look for things that are the same.*
Contrast *means to look for things that are different.*

To solve the riddles in each box, read the clues in the horse.
Then write the letters in the blanks with the matching numbers.

What kind of food does a racehorse like to eat?

___ ___ ___ ___   ___ ___ ___ ___
11 5 10 3   11 9 9 2

1. What letter is in LOG, but not in DOG?
2. What letter is in DIME, but not in TIME?
3. What letter is in BITE, but not in BIKE?
4. What letter is in WEST, but not in REST?
5. What letter is in FAN, but not in FUN?
6. What letter is in BOX, but not in FOX?
7. What letter is in CAR, but not in CAN?
8. What letter is in ME, but not in MY?
9. What letter is in SOCK, but not in SACK?
10. What letter is in SEE, but not in BEE?
11. What letter is in FULL, but not in PULL?

What does a rose sleep in at night?

___ ___ ___ ___ ___ ___   ___ ___ ___
11 1 9 4 8 7   6 8 2

Scholastic Professional Books

Twins

Holly and Polly are twins. They are in the first grade. They look just alike, but they are very different. Holly likes to play softball and soccer. She likes to wear her hair braided when she goes out to play. She wears sporty clothes. Recess is her favorite part of school. Polly likes to read books and paint pictures. Every day she wears a ribbon in her hair to match her dress. Her favorite thing about school is going to the library. She wants to be a teacher some day.

Look at the pictures of Holly and Polly. Their faces look alike. Circle the things in both pictures that are different from each other.

Draw two lines under the words that tell what Holly and Polly do that is the same.

They play sports.   They love to paint.   They are in the first grade.

 Write rhyming names for twins that are boys. What is alike about them? What is different?

Soldier Dads

Juan's dad and Ann's dad are soldiers. Juan's dad is a captain in the Navy. He sails on the ocean in a large ship. Ann's dad is a pilot in the Air Force. He flies a jet. Juan and Ann miss their dads when they are gone for a long time. They write them letters and send them pictures. It is a happy day when their dads come home!

Draw a ☺ in the column under the correct dad. Some sentences may describe both dads.

	Juan's dad	Ann's dad	Both dads
1. He is a captain.			
2. He works on a ship.			
3. Sometimes he is gone for a long time.			
4. He is a pilot.			
5. His child writes to him.			
6. He is in the Air Force.			
7. He is in the Navy.			
8. It is a happy time when he comes home.			
9. He flies a jet.			
10. He is a soldier.			

Dinosaur Clues

How do we know that dinosaurs were real? It is because their bones have been found in rocks. Sometimes scientists have found dinosaur footprints where mud later turned to stone. These kinds of rocks are called fossils. Fossils give us clues about how big the dinosaurs were. Some were small and some were very large. Scientists say a diplodocus was as big as three school buses!

1. Color the picture that shows scientists working.

2. Color the picture of a fossil.

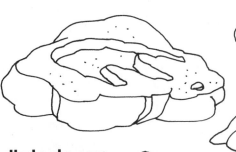

3. Color the picture of a diplodocus.

 Find and write the names of three more dinosaurs.

Amazing Animal Facts

Read each sentence. Then color the picture that tells the meaning of the underlined word.

1. Sea lions sleep in the water with one <u>flipper</u> up in the air.

an arm like a paddle   a beak   a feather

2. Even though whale sharks are the biggest fish in the world, they are <u>harmless</u> to people.

reddish brown   not dangerous   very tiny

3. Horses use their tails to <u>swat</u> pesky flies.

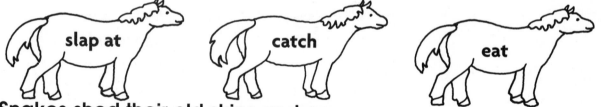

slap at   catch   eat

4. Snakes <u>shed</u> their old skins and grow new ones.

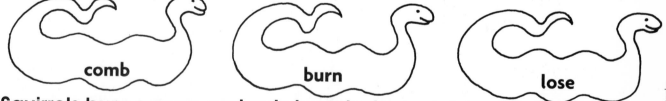

comb   burn   lose

5. Squirrels <u>bury</u> acorns and nuts to eat when winter comes.

bake   hide in the ground   steal

Write an interesting fact about two other animals.

A Tiny Town

Have you ever seen a prairie dog town? That's where <u>prairie dogs</u> live, but there are no buildings or houses. They live underground. They dig deep into the dirt making <u>burrows</u>. Along the  burrows, here and there, are <u>chambers</u> for sleeping or storing food. One chamber is lined with grass for the babies. Sometimes prairie dogs have <u>pests</u> in their town, like rattlesnakes!

Use the code below to learn what some of the words in the story mean. Copy the matching letters in the blanks.

1. town

2. prairie dogs

3. burrows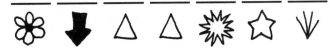

4. chambers

5. unwanted guests

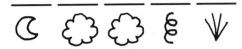

A	C	E	F	I	L	M	N	O	P	R	S	T	U	Y

Name _____

Oops!

 *In a story, there is usually a reason something happens. This is the **cause**. What happens as a result is the **effect**.*

Sandy went on a vacation in the mountains with her parents and little brother Austin. They were staying in a small cabin without any electricity or running water. It was fun to have lanterns at night and to bathe in the cold mountain stream. The biggest problem for Sandy was she missed her best friend, Kendra. Sandy found her dad's cell phone and called Kendra. They talked for nearly an hour! When Sandy's dad went to call his office, the cell phone was dead. He was NOT a happy camper!

Draw a line to match the first part of each sentence to the second part that makes it true.

1. **Sandy used lanterns at night because**

2. **Sandy and Austin bathed in a stream because**

3. **Sandy felt better about missing Kendra because**

4. **Sandy's dad could not call his office because**

she talked to her on the cell phone.

the cabin had no running water.

the cabin had no electricity.

the cell phone was dead.

Write about something you did that caused a huge "effect."

Scholastic Professional Books

Wanda Wiggleworm

*In a story, there is usually a reason something happens. This is the **cause**. What happens as a result is the **effect**.*

Wanda Wiggleworm was tired of living alone in the flowerpot, so she decided to live it up. Last night, Wanda went to the Ugly Bug Ball. She looked her best, all slick and slimy. Carl Caterpillar asked her to dance. They twisted and wiggled around and around to the music. All of a sudden, they got tangled up. They tried to get free, but instead, they tied themselves in a knot! What would they do? They decided to get married, and they lived happily ever after.

Unscramble each sentence about the story.
Write the new sentence on the line.

tangled	worms	when	got	danced.	they	The	up

_____

_____

in	knot	They	married.	a	they	were	so	got	tied

_____

_____

Tim fell asleep on his raft while playing in the lake. Draw a picture of what you think the effect was on Tim.

Name _____

School Rules

It is important to follow the rules at school. Read each rule below. Find the picture that shows what would happen if students DID NOT follow that rule. Write the letter of the picture in the correct box.

1. You must walk, not run, in the halls. ☐

2. Do not chew gum at school. ☐

3. Come to school on time. ☐

4. When the fire alarm rings, follow the leader outside. ☐

5. Listen when the teacher is talking. ☐

6. Keep your desk clean. ☐

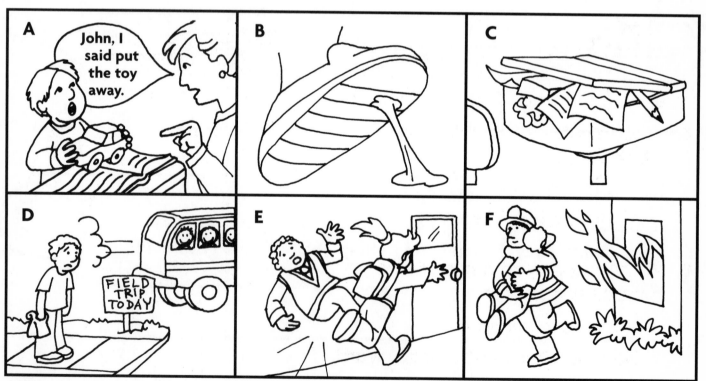

 Write a school rule that you must obey. Draw a picture of what might happen if you do not.

Scholastic Professional Books

Mixed-Up Margie

 A character is a person or animal in a story. To help readers understand a character better, a story often gives details about the character.

Once upon a time there was a mixed-up queen named Margie. She got things mixed up. She wore her crown on her arm. She wore a shoe on her head. She painted every fingernail a different color. Then she painted her nose red! She used a fork to hold her hair in place. She wore a purple belt around her knees. The king didn't mind. He always wore his clothes backward!

Use the story and your crayons to help you follow these instructions:

1. Draw Margie's crown.
2. Draw her shoe.
3. Paint her fingernails and nose.
4. Draw what goes in her hair.
5. Draw her belt.

Circle the correct answer:

6. What makes you think Margie is mixed up?

   the way she dresses

   the way she talks

7. What makes you think the king is mixed up, too?

   He talks backward.

   He wears his clothes backward.

 Pretend tomorrow is Mixed-Up Day. Describe what you will wear as a mixed-up character.

Scholastic Professional Books

Miss Ticklefoot

I love Miss Ticklefoot. She is my first-grade teacher.

To find out more about her, read each sentence below. Write a word in each blank that tells how she feels. The Word Box will help you.

Word Box

sad	scared	silly	worried	happy	surprised

1. Miss Ticklefoot smiles when we know the answers.

_____

2. She is concerned when one of us is sick.

_____

3. She makes funny faces at us during recess.

_____

4. She cried when our fish died.

_____

5. She jumps when the fire alarm rings.

_____

6. Her mouth dropped open when we gave her a present!

_____

Different Friends

When Ty was four years old, he had two make-believe friends named Mr. Go-Go and Mr. Sasso. They lived in Ty's closet. When there was no one else around, Ty talked to Mr. Go-Go while he played with his toys. Mr. Go-Go was a good friend. He helped put Ty's toys away. Mr. Sasso was not a good friend. Some days he forgot to make Ty's bed or brush Ty's teeth. One day he even talked back to Ty's mother. Another day Dad said, "Oh my! Who wrote on the wall?" Ty knew who did it . . . Mr. Sasso!

Read the phrase inside each crayon. If it describes Mr. Go-Go, color it green. If it describes Mr. Sasso, color it red. If it describes both, color it yellow.

1. helpful

2. probably sassy

3. forgets to do chores

4. friends that live in the closet

5. could get Ty in trouble

6. make-believe characters

7. does the right thing

Draw Mr. Go-Go.

Draw Mr. Sasso.

Write something you think Mr. Sasso and Mr. Go-Go might do.

Scholastic Professional Books

Poetry

A poem paints a picture with words. It often uses rhyming words.

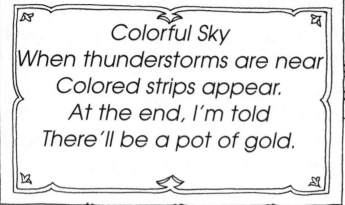

Colorful Sky
When thunderstorms are near
Colored strips appear.
At the end, I'm told
There'll be a pot of gold.

Draw what it is.

1. Draw a red line under the word that rhymes with <u>near</u>.

2. Draw a green line under the word that rhymes with <u>told</u>.

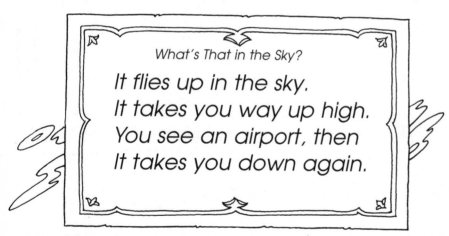

What's That in the Sky?

It flies up in the sky.
It takes you way up high.
You see an airport, then
It takes you down again.

Draw what it is.

3. Draw a blue circle around the word that rhymes with <u>sky</u>.

4. Draw a brown circle around the word that rhymes with <u>then</u>.

5. Finish this two-line poem:

I wish that I could see

A giant bumble_____.

Draw what it is.

Now see if you can make up your own two-line poem using these rhyming words at the end of each line: G0 and SNOW.

Scholastic Professional Books

A Fable

A fable is a story that teaches a lesson. This fable was written many, many years ago.

The Dog and His Shadow

A dog carried a piece of meat in his mouth. He crossed over a river on a low bridge. He looked down into the water and saw his reflection. It looked like another dog with a piece of meat larger than his. The dog snapped at the other dog's meat. When he did, his own meat dropped into the water. Now the dog didn't have any meat at all.

Draw a box around the lesson that the story teaches:

1. **Two dogs are better than one.**

2. **Don't be greedy. Be happy with what you have.**

Color only the pictures of things that you read about in the story:

  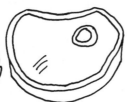 

Write a complete sentence telling what the dog should have done.

Library Books

 A library has many different kinds of books.

It is fun to check books out of the library. Have you ever read *Rainbow Fish* by Marcus Pfister? It is a story about a very special fish. His scales were blue, green, and purple. He also had some shiny, silver scales. The other fish wanted him to share his shiny scales with them, but he said no. No one would be his friend. Later, he decided to give each fish one of his shiny scales. It was better to lose some of his beauty and have friends than to keep them to himself.

Connect the dots. You will see something from the book.

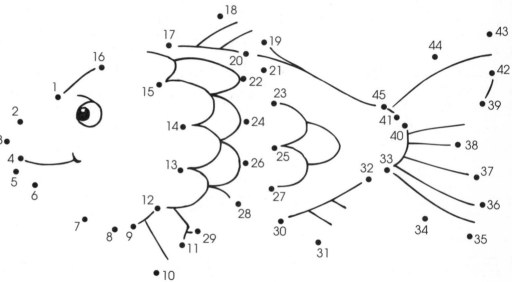

1. Draw a blue circle around the word that tells what this book is about:

     running   lying   sharing   eating

2. Copy the name of the author here.

_____

- -

_____

If you grew up to be an author, what would you write about? Make a pretty book cover that includes the title of your book.

Scholastic Professional Books

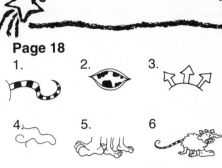

Page 4
1. a good reader; 2. looks at the picture; 3. the title; 4. the words

Page 5
Main idea: Trucks do important work.

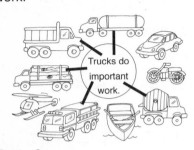

Page 6
Main idea: Clowns can do funny tricks.

Page 7
KATE: Names have special meanings.

Casey means brave.
George means farmer.
Sarah means princess.

Page 8

Page 9

1. in reading class; 2. camping

Page 10
Kelly packed pajamas, shirt, shorts, toothbrush, toothpaste, hairbrush, swimsuit, pillow, storybooks, sunglasses. Compound words: grandmother, suitcase, toothbrush, toothpaste, hairbrush, swimsuit, storybooks, sunglasses

Page 11
1. Texas; 2. oil; 3. President; 4. wife; 5. Jenna
His cat's name is INDIA.

Page 12
Make-believe: ketchup bottles and a watermelon bowling, a talking milk jug, dancing bananas, chicken wings that can fly all by themselves, laughing soup cans, dancing carrots

Page 13
Facts: Clouds float in the sky. Clouds are made of tiny drops of water. Fog is a cloud on the ground. (All others are make-believe.)

Page 14
5, 1; 4, 3, 2
Tara bought pencils, scissors, glue, and crayons.

Page 15
6, 4, 2; 3, 1, 5
LEARN TO DIVE

Page 16
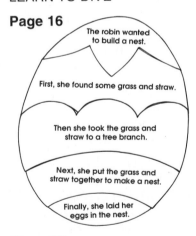

Page 17
1. Each star should be outlined in blue and colored red inside. 2. One moon should be yellow and one orange. 3. A face should be drawn on each sun. 4. 3; 5. 2; 6. 4; 7. 3 + 2 + 4 = 9; 8. stars moon

Page 18
1. 2. 3. 4. 5. 6

Page 19
The pictures that do not belong are bike, telephone, snowman, pumpkin, skates, and frog. (The other pictures should be colored.)
2. hot, cold; 3. up, down; 4. starfish; 5. yellow

Page 20
IT WAS A FLYING CARPET. No

Page 21
1. true; 2. false; 3. false; 4. true; 5. true

Page 22
The children's pictures should include everything described in the sentences.

Page 23
The children should have added these things to the picture: black clouds, lightning striking the tallest tree, the word "Moo" in a bubble above a cow, rain, a mud puddle by the barn door, hay blowing out of the barn window.

Page 24
1. penguin; 2. baby; 3. octopus; 4. ant; 5. grandmother; 6. bear; 7. firefighter

Page 25
1. chickenpox; 2. James scratched them. 3. 9; 4. She got chickenpox, too.

Page 26

Page 27

Bacon and eggs do not belong.

Page 28

Sandie's Shoe Store: sandals, boots, sneakers, high heels; Movie Town Cinema: tickets, popcorn, big screen, candy; Pepe's Mexican Food: tacos, burrito, beans, peppers; Gale's Gardening Goodies: tulip bulbs, fertilizer, gardening gloves, pots

Page 29

Meats: ham, chicken, roast; Dairy: milk, cheese, yogurt; Bread: rolls, bagels, biscuits; Fruits and Vegetables: carrots, corn, apples

Page 30

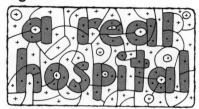

Page 31

He knew he had to do the right thing.

Page 32

FAST FOOD, FLOWER BED

Page 33

They are in the first grade.

Page 34

1. Juan's dad; 2. Juan's dad; 3. both; 4. Ann's dad; 5. both; 6. Ann's dad; 7. Juan's dad; 8. both; 9. Ann's dad; 10. both

Page 35

Page 36

1. an arm like a paddle; 2. not dangerous; 3. slap at; 4. lose; 5. hide in the ground

Page 37

1. a small city; 2. little furry animals; 3. tunnels; 4. rooms; 5. pests

Page 38

1. Sandy used lanterns at night because the cabin had no electricity. 2. Sandy and Austin bathed in a stream because the cabin had no running water. 3. Sandy felt better about missing Kendra because she talked to her on the cell phone. 4. Sandy's dad could not call his office because the cell phone was dead.

Page 39

1. The worms got tangled up when they danced. 2. They were tied in a knot so they got married.

Page 40

1. E; 2. B; 3. D; 4. F; 5. A; 6. C

Page 41

The children's pictures should show a crown on Margie's arm, a shoe on her head, different colors on each fingernail, a red nose, a fork in her hair, and a purple belt around her knees.

6. the way she dresses; 7. He wears his clothes backward.

Page 42

1. happy; 2. worried; 3. silly; 4. sad; 5. scared; 6. surprised

Page 43

1. green; 2. red; 3. red; 4. yellow; 5. red; 6. yellow; 7. green

Page 44

Picture: rainbow 1. appear; 2. gold; Picture: airplane 3. high; 4. again; 5. bee

Page 45

2. Don't be greedy. Be happy with what you have. Picture answers: dog, meat, bridge

Page 46

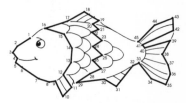

1. sharing 2. Marcus Pfister